Reflections

Peter McDermott

BookLeaf
Publishing

Presentation by *BookLeaf Publishing*

Web: www.bookleafpub.com

E-mail: info@bookleafpub.com

ISBN: 9789357440424

First edition 2023

This first book of mine is dedicated to all those who see things in me that I sometimes fail to see in myself, those that encourage and walk with me on the journey.

And to my wife who always supports, loves and strengthens me.

PREFACE

I've been thinking about trying to get into writing for some time now. This book is a compilation of 21 different poems that I've written. They vary in composition, style and tone, but all are about subjects close to my heart. Some are more light-hearted and humourous, others are deep introspective works. All are written to make us think about and look the world in different ways. I hope you find some encouragement inspiration from reading and absorbing these poems.

The Water's on the rise

Waves upon the ocean
Ripples on the Sea
The flowing river's endless journey
Which Direction will it take?

Through cities towns and villages
Wherever hearts may roam
The river winds and twists its way
Along the journey home

Shadows on the horizon
Storm clouds shroud the sky
Death for some, life for others
The Water's on the rise

Paths and fields, homes and lives
Are lost beneath the flood
The World is changed, but hope remains
Despite the cost of blood

Eventually clouds roll away
The light breaks through at last
But death has shown its icy hand
The sorrow hasn't past

What lies beneath is lost forever
The water rages on
Yet life, and light and love remain
Hope is not yet gone

The flood finally subsides
Dark waters drain away
What's left is different, broken, hurting
But ushers in a brand new day

Our world is dark and drowning
Hope seems forever lost
Full of darkness, depths and raging seas
Are we sure it's worth the cost?

The Sharpened Knife

Metal scapes on metal
It screams, screeches, grinds and aches
Its teeth are readied for action

Scape follows scrape
Screech follows screech
Grind follows grind

Metal glints in the sunlight
As darkness falls, the moonlight takes over
It casts an eerie, evil glow along its jagged face

The rosewood handle's brown like earth,
Red like blood
It holds the blade in a vice-like, death-like grip

The glistening blade, the earthen handle
A deadly duo, contained within a blackened
sheath
Tool in one man's hand, harbinger of death in
anothers

Tool or killer, the knife cares not
All it knows and wills is to hear its master's call

The nature of the master's heart
Decides the blades destiny
Murderer or saint, prophet, poet, pilgrim, healer,
killer.

Until the moment of decision,
Handle, blade and sheath rest in uneasy silence,
Waiting, listening.

The word is spoken,
The handle grasped
Blackened sheath falls away
Flash of light, clang of metal.

A decision rashly taken
A precious life ended.
Gleaming blade darkened forever,
A destiny unveiled.

God went for a walk one day:
(The founding of the Church)

God went for a walk one day
Through trees and fields of green
Alone, at peace, yet troubled.
Beneath a turquoise sky.

It isn't good, the Lord decided,
To walk in solitude
A place, a people, set apart, was what His heart
desired.

A people that are mine to mould,
A place that bears my name
A beacon, and an endless chain
To reach a hurting world

Strength and vision, they will have
But also stubbornness and pride
Yet mine alone they will remain
And I will love them still

To east and west I'll send them out
In my name and power
They'll reap, and sow and spread my word
My heart within their souls

They'll often stumble in the dark
And fall and fail and struggle
They'll even fight amongst themselves
But still, I'll love them so.

One day they'll find their tasks fulfilled
And I shall call them home
They'll walk beside me through the trees
And rest beside the stream

Darkness resides

Darkness resides where the shadows fall
When light is gone and hope is lost

Darkness resides where hearts are cold
When men retreat and turn their heads

Darkness resides where we think of ourselves
Before our brothers and those in need

Darkness resides where hunger burns
When life is cruel and we are alone

Darkness resides where faith departs
In life, in love, in hope, in us

Yet hope resides beside us still
It waits, it knocks and calls us home

The Dark King

A tower, beast and body
A cell, a gravestone, an axe

Death flows from mind and hands and pen
stroke

Obsession, hatred, psychotic rage
But also hope and brotherhood

A mind like a razor, soul of a poet
Dark thoughts, tempered yet accentuated by
adventure

A throne, a fortune, obtained through blood
Creator and destroyer
Darkening imagination, becoming darker still

His creation, cast upon the wind
Drawn into the hearts of others
Moulded, changed, adapted and set adrift once
more

But, yet the dark creator is angered by his own
creation.

A past sometimes shrouded,
A future drenched in crimson
The ruler draws his subjects near
His blade is now unsheathed

A doctor
A killer
A King

Trio of Limericks

There once was a man from the sea
Whose name began with a C
His name is a joke
And rather bespoke
Because at the end of his name was a T

The young lady was rather aggressive
Her husband was mildly possessive
They owned a large dog
That looked like a hog
And whose affection was often concussive

Do you remember that man from Nantucket?
He's still got his head in a bucket
It may be cliché
But at the end of the day
If you don't like it then... nevermind

I went to church this morning

I went to church this morning
I didn't want to go
Wearily, I raised my head
And said let's start this show

I stumbled through the bedroom door
And headed down the stairs
Stubbed my toe and banged my head
And tried to hold the swears

My morning wasn't going well
I wish I'd stayed in bed
I tried to make myself some toast
Of course I'm out of bread

So, hungry and defeated
Is how this day begins
The bus flies, by, I try to run
The driver only laughs

More through luck than judgement
I made it there at last
A smile, a hug and open hearts
Their love and faith steadfast

I slept through the announcements
I slumbered through the hymns
I napped throughout the sermon
My chance of heavens grim

Folk around me tut and stare
As I wake up again
I had a plan to save myself
I bowed and said Amen

Those that saw me sleeping
Thought I had been in prayer
I had to make my exit fast
Before my lies ensnare

Sheepishly I made my way
And slunk towards the door
"Feel free to sleep" the minister said
"But please try not to snore"

The wind keeps blowing

The wind keeps blowing through the night
The trees creak and moan
Is sleep forever lost to me?
The moon casts an ungodly, profane glow
Angry shadows dance like soulless demons
The wind keeps blowing

The wind keeps blowing
A branch snaps, crashes against my window
Relentless and violent rain cascades from an
obsidian sky
Lightening flashes and streaks and blazes
through the midnight ether
The wind keeps blowing

The wind keeps blowing
In that single, brief, shining glimmering instant
The world is illuminated,
Then darkness returns and swallows the light
Infinite, darkness, endless shadows
The wind keeps blowing

Leave me be

I'm sitting on my ass today
And I'm not getting up
I've been at work, I haven't stopped
So that's it, leave me be

I don't care if it rains or snows
If lightening flashes or thunder cracks
I'm sitting on my ass all day
So that's it, leave me be

If the world around me blows away
Or waters rise and reach the sky
Still I'll be sitting warm and dry
So that's it, leave me be

There's nothing anyone can do or say
I will not move an inch
I've had enough, I've done my bit
So that's it, leave me be

Looking out across the ocean

I looked out across the azure ocean
Waiting and watching
For what, I did not know
Still I waited, still I watched

As wave followed wave I kept my silent watch
A sentinel at the gates of a mighty citadel
Still I waited, still I watched

A marbled boulder, beaten and chiseled by time
and tide became my watchtower
Still I waited, still I watched

Endlessly the waves continue their march,
Ever onwards, like a mighty, immeasurable
army
But futile was their advance
Still I waited, still I watched

Each time the waves approached
Despite the ferocity of each attack
They faltered, halted and collapsed
Still I waited, still I watched

Blue skies turned to burning red and orange

Eventually fading to a shadowy grey
The waves still continued their endless doomed
advance
Still I waited, still I watched

The light vanished completely
But darkness will not restrain or slow their
tireless assault
Still I waited, still I watched

The air grew colder, life flashed
Decisions taken, opportunities gone by
That will never come this way again
Loves and loss, victories, defeats.
On and on they came like the waves themselves
Still I waited, still I watched

Visions, echoes of what was, what could have
been, and that will never be
This endless march will never stop
Still I wait, still I watch

Journey through the darkness

I walk alone through the city streets
The light begins to dim
People rush by trying to make their way home
Before darkness engulfs the world

Shop front windows clatter shut
Natural light is extinguished
The Orange glow of street lights take over
As the void moves ever closer to completing its
dark design

The streets begin to empty, occasional light from
windows catches my eye
As I continue my journey into the night
And as the night continues Its journey into me

One by one lights from houses begin to vanish
The whole world seems to be drifting off into
peaceful oblivion
No such luck for me
I must face the nights full yet silent fury

The moonlight fails me
As black, ashen clouds obscure it from view
Like a great, dark hand reaching out, grasping it

And tearing it from the heavens

The street lights flicker, until they too lose their fight against the nights oppressive malevolent march

Still I wander, darkness within and without
As the moonlight was devoured
So too are the stars themselves swallowed up,
Only the endless void remains

A clatter and a clash behind me makes me momentarily halt my journey through the shadows
I shudder and turn towards the noise
Only the void meets my terrified gaze
Endless darkness, the world seems lost
Taken and replaced by emptiness

I keep my slow and steady pace,
Footsteps echo in the silence
Almost as loud as my pounding heart
Beating as a great thunderous, deafening drum

Footsteps and heartbeat seem to work in unison
Warning of what's to come, the violence of this endless night

Boom and thud, boom and thud

Growing ever louder
Boom and bust, boom and thud
Louder still, and faster
Boom and thud, boom and thud
Sweat drips, fists clench, hairs stand up, eyes
widen in terror
My body has realised what my heart fears to
even comprehend

I am not alone

Voice in the night

Daylight is shrouded and completely consumed
The night encompasses all
Alone, I look, I watch, I stare
A whisper barely noticed drifts through the air

I question my senses, I ask who approaches
Silence returns, stillness unbroken
But something remains, a ghost or a phantom
A wraith or a spirit, or just my heart's fearful
anthem

It was definitely there! I heard it I felt it.
That still, muted voice from within or without
Shapeless and formless yet palpably real
Sailed by on the breeze
Some great truth yet to reveal

Archangel or demon, friend or imposter
Servant or master, hero or villain
I must have an answer, what secrets are hidden
This voice stirs my soul and drives my ambition

Through the stillness and quiet and peace of the
night
The maddening voice returns, for an instant

Then drifts on again and escapes from my grasp
Then encircles, examines and lingers at last

What do you want of me voice in the night?
Do you comfort, convict, inspire or deter?
Are you ally or enemy, granting hope or despair?
"Come closer and listen" it said "if you dare"

"I am the voice of all that you are,
I am all that you hope for, all that you fear
all of your triumphs and all your despair
I'm beside you, within you, I know you beware!"

The void and the shadow

The void and the shadow stare into my soul
And I glare back into a deep endless holes
"You'll never break me" cries a great booming
voice
"But fight me and challenge me, if that is your
choice"

A great battle ensues, between myself and the
shadow
We charge and we grapple, blow follows blow
We all face this battle at times in our lives
To decide who we are, whether goodness
survives

The shadow's this world, and our darkest intent
We fight for our souls, how are lives will be
spent
Goodness or darkness, both hang in the balance
Your choice, your design, what to do with your
talents

If the shadow succeeds, then hope will be lost
You must not give up, whatever the cost
Our souls are so precious, and of course worth
the fight
Do not let your hearts be swallowed by night

Mary's not just a little girl

Mary's not just a little girl
Who had a snow white lamb
She had God's word within her heart
A keystone of His plan

The lamb was under Mary's care
Until He came of age
And then He wandered here and there
To free us from our cage

He gathered those around Him
Inspired men with His word
Sowed seeds of love and justice
And blessed all those who heard

Eventually He made His way
To a hill called Calvary
With anguished heart and dying breath
He thought of you and me

Death was not the end of course
Though His enemies thought it was
He rose and lives and walks with us
Death has lost its claws

The battle

The light has vanished, I run to the tower
I take my place with great men of power
They think I'm scared, but I stand my ground
I raise my voice though heart beat pounds

This is my place, I have a voice
I won't back down, I've made my choice
There are times to follow and times to lead
The day is mine, I'm strong indeed

An army approaches that will not yield
The king comes forth with sword and with
shield
He bids us all to gird ourselves
To prepare for war, and ring out the bells

We stand together to face this foe
Yet great lords and ladies think me slow
I've worked hard and trained to gain all my
power
This is my time, this is my hour

The army crashes and smashes the gate
What happens next is up to fate
Some will stand and others falter

Some must die and lie on the altar

My course is set, my courage strong
But those great men, their strength is gone
So never doubt my size or my heart
I'll hold my own and play my heart

The battles done, many lie broken
Armour rent and treasures stolen
Yet the fortress and, kingdom still it remains
Never doubt my strength again

For those that have gone before

I took a walk amongst the graves
Of those that went before me
The dear departed souls of those
Who walk this earth no more

Rows of crosses and marble stones
That mark where they now rest
Yet peace and hope are what I find
As I walk past the fallen

So many lives, and so much loss
Yet why do I find peace?
Because amongst the grief and pain
Their stories echo on

All were loved and all were lost
These folk from yesterday
They laughed and wept, felt pain and joy
We must hear what they still say

They speak of what once was,
What will not be again
Teary eyed we think of those
Who we once walked beside

Names etched in stone surround me
Their simple epitaphs
A lifetimes worth of loved ones thoughts
Summed up in simple verse

Beloved one, sincerely missed
Until we meet again
Simple words yet deeply felt
Great truths that help us on

This world was theirs, these friends of ours
They made our lives worthwhile
And now they walk ahead of us
And we must stay behind

Of all the things they could bequeath
To those of us that linger on
The best of course is each new day
Precious time that we must seize

This world is ours, for us to shape
Though their loss has left it colder
Yet each wise word and each kind thought
Will never leave our hearts

And so I walk amongst these graves
Of those that went before
I'll carry on what you began
You still live within my soul

My muddy shoes and footprints

My muddy shoes and footprints
I earned with every step
A longing for adventure
Made me start my epic quest

My journey started, as they often do
With one foot out the door
Of course there's no way I could know
What my wanderings had in store

Through bitter cold, and pouring rain
And summers blazing heat
I walked, I strolled I even ran
And marched with blistered feet

I had no destination
When I set out that day
The journey is its own reward
I repeated all the way

Footstep followed footstep
Something calls me ever on
Strange forces are at work today
Some unseen paragon

Mile after mile
Is swallowed by my endless walk
When will I get to rest again
Overhead a raven squawks

There's no more looking back for me
I don't think I can stop
I have to keep on moving forward
And march until I drop

To colossal heights and cavernous depths
And all that lies between
What more is out there to be found?
What dangers unforseen?

Throughout all my wanderings
Through adventures good and bad
I realise what I sought the most
Was what I always had

A home and peace within my soul
Was what I went searching for
Of course I now know every step
Just took me further from my door

In the morning when I rise

In the morning when I rise
A new day greets my eyes
Some days I wish it'd wait awhile
Before sunlight lights the skies

Some days I feel I've had enough
When life's overtly tough
But then I have to tell myself
I'm made of sterner stuff

My heart is steel, my eyes blaze true
I'll see this challenge through
In the morning when I rise
My dreams I will pursue

Fallen kingdom

Ring the bells and blow the horns
The king is on his way
People crowd the streets to see
His glory passing by

But all that gold and splendor
Is nothing but a show
He wants the world to see him
As he wished he saw himself

He's broken up inside his heart
He has no more to give
He plans to live, but hopes to die
His world is crashing down

His face is set with forced delight
But his eyes reveal the lie
How can a man with power and wealth be so
downcast and lost?

He sees the end is coming soon
For this kingdom that he rules
He plays the part that he must play
And hides the bitter truth

His enemies are multiplying
Both from inside and out
Cracks that have been hidden well
Won't stay silent anymore

These people that surround him now
Are all condemned to die
He wishes he could tell them all
What fate will soon dispense

Not by violent army,
Or by flaming arrow fire
Their deaths will creep upon them all
When they all least suspect

Gold and jewels will not protect
Nor iron gates defend
The king is bringing death himself
To all those who surround

Procrastination

I really should go up to bed
The day has long since gone
If I'm up any later
Then the new day will be here

There's so much that I planned to do
This evening before I rest
But life has taken all my strength
And trampled my desire

I've sat alone and searched my heart
For answer to my apathy
And all that I've discovered is
I've wasted so much time

Some make the most of each new hour
Cape Diem is their cry
But I just do not seem to have
That bright internal flame

My eyes are growing heavy
My limbs just want respite
But my mind is having none of that
It seeks the answer still

That fire within's not truly out
Unless we give power to fear
We all have strength within ourselves
Even if it's buried deep

So now I'm heading off to bed
But know that I'm not beat
Tomorrow is another day
And I will make it mine

Milton Keynes UK
Ingram Content Group UK Ltd.
UKHW020728301023
431584UK00015B/779